CW00551098

QUILT
AUSTRALIA

£2.99

37 ¼

Oz Icon (Pl. 16) Wendy Holland

QUILT
AUSTRALIA

THE QUILTERS' GUILD

BAY BOOKS
Sydney London

DEDICATION

The Quilters' Guild would like to dedicate this book to the exhibitors whose quilts were damaged by a fire at the photographer's studio in 1987. They are: Lois Densham; Sally Evers; Dianne Finnegan; Judith Fluke and Roy Fluke; Helen Macartney; Barbara Macey; Cynthia Morgan; Elsie Morrison; D. Anne Neal; Marie Parnell; Holly Pittman; Wendy Saclier and Vivienne Mildren; Prue Socha; Phyllis Sullivan; Crazy Cooperative: Sue Bach, Ruth Caple, Christine Cemm, Dorothy De Nys, Marle Popple, Jos Tolson; Dubbo Patchwork and Quilters' Group: Fay Bifhoff, Charlene Bower, Elizabeth Charlston, Meg Corish, Janice Garth, Cis Honner, Suzanne Laird, Louise Martel, Cheryl Pratter, Naomi Raison, Alicia Rawson, Susan Tooth, Julie Vaughn, Joanne Webb.

This publication has been funded by the
Bicentennial Women's Program of the
Australian Bicentennial Authority.

This book is copyright. Apart from any fair dealing for the purpose of private study, research, criticism or review, as permitted under the Copyright Act, no part may be reproduced by any process without written permission. Enquiries should be addressed to the publishers.

Published by Bay Books, 61-69 Anzac Parade,
Kensington, NSW 2033

Publisher: George Barber

Copyright © The Quilters' Guild Inc.

National Library of Australia
Card number and ISBN 1 86256 260 1

Designed by Susan Kinealy

Photography by Karl Schwerdtfeger — D4 DOG, except
where otherwise acknowledged

Postscript photography by amateurs except where
otherwise acknowledged

Typesetting by Savage Type Pty Ltd

Printed in Singapore by Toppan Printing Co.

Front cover: *Rainbow Serpent at the Opera House* (Pl. 32) Helen Slocombe
Back cover: *Unchanging Hues* (Pl. 79) Dianne Johnston
Endpaper: Detail *Sail Away* (Pl. 12) Diana Goulston Robinson

CONTENTS

Plate 1 *Hexagon Quilt* c.1840 attributed to Elizabeth Macarthur, Parramatta, NSW. 285 × 272 cm
Collection: National Trust of Australia, NSW. Photograph courtesy of the Historic Houses Trust of New South Wales

FOREWORD

Over the past couple of decades there has been a revival of interest in traditional crafts throughout Australia. This interest and activity has been given greater impetus by the celebration of the Bicentenary of European settlement of Australia.

Greater public awareness of the so-called 'lesser'arts , often the domain of women, and a determination not to let seldom practised arts die out, have also played their part. Attention paid by collectors, scholars, art gallery and museum staff to these previously less fashionable domestic or 'folk' arts, has also contributed to their popularity. There are now collectors, public and private, of vernacular pottery; decorated, rustic and primitive furniture; and textile art, including embroidery, patchwork and quiltmaking.

Exhibitions such as 'Colonial Crafts of Victoria' at the National Gallery of Victoria in 1978, and 'Crafts of South Australia' at the Art Gallery of South Australia in 1986, and numerous articles and publications, have documented objects of all kinds and stimulated many people to find out more, and often try a variety of decorative arts and crafts themselves.

Although the art of patchwork and quiltmaking has always been part of Australia's craft tradition, it has certainly been revived in recent years. This revival probably owes something to a similar revival of the art in the USA, in 1976, when America celebrated the Bicentenary of its Independence. There, a long and lively tradition was greatly invigorated by the attention focused on it. Numerous exhibitions and publications further spread the word throughout the USA and internationally.

Life in Australia was hard for the early settlers. Women, as well as men, were often employed clearing bush, ploughing paddocks and herding cattle. At the end of the day women still had to do their housekeeping and for many, there was seldom the opportunity for creative work like patchwork and quiltmaking. Because Australia does not have a long snow-bound winter, time given to these arts was further reduced.

Many women, however, did manage to devote some time to beautifying their homes, even where life was hard. The walls were decorated with pictures saved from illustrated newspapers; rag rugs were often hooked from scraps of worn-out clothing, and patchwork quilts patiently sewn to brighten up the bed. Those who were better off and had more leisure time, kept scrapbooks, painted and decorated furniture, and practised embroidery, patchwork and quiltmaking.

Today the revival of interest in all forms of needlework has reached deep into the community, especially as women, increasingly freed from time-consuming housework, have sought greater creative satisfaction. Needlework has become one of the most popular domestic arts because it is relatively inexpensive and easy to learn. Guided by articles in magazines, specialist publications and other quiltmakers, diverse groups of people throughout Australia practise the arts of needlework. The long-established embroiderers' guilds in each state, and the flourishing Quilters' Guild, with a national membership, attest to their Australia-wide popularity.

The Quilt Australia '88 project, organised by The Quilters' Guild, comprises exhibitions and activities that focus further attention on quilts and quiltmaking throughout the community. Quiltmakers across Australia have submitted their work for selection and inclusion in the exhibitions. The variety and richness of their work cannot fail to impress.

JOHN MCPHEE
SENIOR CURATOR, AUSTRALIAN ART
AUSTRALIAN NATIONAL GALLERY
SEPTEMBER 1987

ACKNOWLEDGEMENTS

The Quilters' Guild gratefully acknowledges assistance given by the following:

The Australian Bicentennial Authority for funding from the Bicentennial Women's Program to publish *Quilt Australia*

The Australia Council, Visual Arts/Craft Board, the Australian Government's Arts Funding and Advisory Body for a development grant to assist the Quilt Australia '88 exhibition

Coats Semco for financial assistance towards the Quilt Australia '88 exhibition

The National Trust of Australia (NSW) for permission to reproduce photographs of the Elizabeth Macarthur quilt

The Historic Houses Trust of New South Wales for the supply of photographs of the Elizabeth Macarthur quilt

The Australian Quilters' Association, Victoria

The Queensland Quilters

The Quilters' Guild of South Australia

The Western Australian Quilters' Association

The Canberra Quilters

The Tasmanian Quilting Guild

Mrs Leigh Taumoefalau

Margaret Rolfe, Glennda Marsh and Annette Gero for advice on historical information

Wendy Holland for advice on contemporary quilts and design

Margot Child for advice and help at all stages

Plate 2 *Medallion Quilt* c.1890-1900 made by Mrs Brown of Bowning, NSW for Margaret Swann. 228 × 182 cm
Collection: Leigh Taumoefalau

10

INTRODUCTION
BACKGROUND TO QUILT AUSTRALIA '88

Detail *Medallion quilt* (Pl. 2)
The Quilt Australia '88 logo

The Quilt Australia '88 exhibition was organised by members of The Quilters' Guild to celebrate Australia's Bicentenary. Three programmes were developed; a national exhibition of contemporary and historic quilts, a schools' Banner project for the children in schools in New South Wales, and a travelling exhibition of small quilts touring the states.

Such an ambitious programme demanded the long-term commitment of a group of women who formed the bicentennial subcommittee of the Guild. Acting in a voluntary capacity, their determination to promote quiltmaking in Australia sustained them through the three years of planning and implementation. Support from Guild members and from quilting associations throughout Australia was essential, and in planning the activities, a communication network was developed between all state guilds.

Whenever expert advice was needed, there was someone within the Guild, or an interested friend, who helped. Many groups and individuals raised money, and everyone contributed by signing Signature quilts and buying Guild T-shirts. Granting bodies and sponsors assisted with funding, and in particular, the Australia Council Visual Arts/Craft Board assisted with the Quilt Australia '88 exhibition and the Suitcase touring exhibition.

'Women's work' is so often ephemeral, and to record the quilts so that they might be enjoyed beyond the exhibition, the book *Quilt Australia* was conceived. With Guild resources stretched, the Australian Bicentennial Authority made a grant toward the publication. The project was enthusiastically received, and the commitment nationwide helped sustain everyone, especially when a fire in the photographer's studio destroyed seventeen of the quilts (see Postscript).

All of the components of the Quilt Australia '88 programme are a credit to the dedication of the project's small subcommittee, the quiltmakers of Australia, and all of the national granting bodies who contributed towards both the exhibition and the book.

With the growth of guilds in each state, the craft has increased greatly in popularity. Most quiltmakers initially worked within the parameters of patterns developed in Britain and the United States. To encourage them to think beyond these influences, and to strive even harder for excellence, the Guild invited all Australian quiltmakers to submit quilts with an Australian theme for a national exhibition.

The entry categories covered many aspects of Australian life; patriotic, political, personal and natural, as well as a traditional category which allowed quiltmakers to interpret established patterns. These categories were suggested only as a framework for exploring new and old ideas.

The response was rich and varied, demonstrating the vitality and competence of Australian quiltmakers. Drawing on the landscape and culture of our country, the colours and shapes in the quilts reflect a confident exploration of Australian identity.

Australia is not without its own heritage of quilts. Even before Europeans came to Australia, the Aborigines were sewing patchwork rugs from the skins of animals (Rolfe, 1987, 14-17). From 1818 to 1843, prison reformer Elizabeth Fry presented each convict woman being transported to the new colony of New South Wales with two pounds of fabric scraps to make a patchwork quilt during her long sea voyage. This was to make the idle hours productive and provide the women with a source of revenue.

Few of the early quilts have survived, probably because of the harsh conditions, and also because few were made. Elizabeth Macarthur's *Hexagon Quilt* (Pl. 1) typifies the English paper method of construction. This technique is still the first many aspiring quiltmakers use. Nancy Tingey, one of the exhibitors, has reinterpreted it (Pl. 66).

Another style that recurs throughout Australia's history is the medallion quilt. A central block surrounded by borders allows

Detail *Hexagon Quilt* (Pl. 1)

Detail *Hanging Red Gum Leaves* (Pl. 66)

for many variations, and the *Medallion Quilt* (Pl. 2), with a central block of an early Australian coat of arms, is a fine example. It was owned by Margaret Swann who lived at Elizabeth Farm early this century (Gero, 1987). The 'turkey red' coat of arms, with stars and surrounded by triangles, on a white background, is the logo for the Guild's Quilt Australia '88 activities. It was chosen for its idiosyncratic interpretation of the Australian coat of arms. The quilt was made before the coat of arms was officially proclaimed, but early versions existed. Surely the quiltmaker enjoyed sewing the shield on upside down, and the emu and kangaroo looking back over their shoulders share the joke.

Many of the quilt styles that flourished were imported. The medallion and hexagon quilts came from Britain, the log cabin and block repeat patterns were widespread in America. However, in the translation of these patterns, they were often given an Australian flavour. For instance, the crazy patch so popular in Victorian times might include embroidered wattle, kangaroos and other identifiably Australian motifs (Rolfe, 1987, 60).

Since World War Two, improved communications and increasing wealth and leisure time resulted in greater access to British and American patchwork traditions. Glennda Marsh (1987) documents several quiltmakers whose initial interest was awakened by books on American or English patchwork. Elisabeth Kruger (Hersey, 1979) taught herself from books, and with increasing technical expertise and confidence, developed her own distinctive designs. Her first exhibition at the Crafts Council of the Australian Capital Territory's gallery in 1978 was a seminal influence, and she has extended this influence by teaching. Barbara Macey is another quiltmaker who worked in isolation for many years. Inspired by the typically American log cabin, she has pushed it into a new dimension. Barbara Macey has always worked as a quilt artist — only one of her quilts has been made specifically to cover a bed (Pl. 102).

The Bicentenary of America's Independence in 1976 provided a tremendous spur for quiltmaking in that country, and Australians living there relayed new developments to other Australian quiltmakers. Trudy Billingsley has made several trips to the United States, and her teaching has

Detail *Postscript to the Dreaming* (Pl. 97)

Detail *Oz Icon* (Pl. 16)

influenced many students of the art to become teachers or prolific quiltmakers. Her work reflects the process of learning new techniques and patterns, then establishing an individual style using the Australian landscape for inspiration.

The emergence of a distinctively Australian approach to quiltmaking was heralded by the publication of several books in this country. First came the 'How to . . .' books, by Margaret Rolfe (1985, 1986) and Deborah Brearley (1985). Patterns in these books use Australian motifs to develop sewing techniques. Barbara Macey and Susan Denton's book (1987) includes chapters on technique and design as well as photographs of contemporary Australian quilts.

Detail *A Sunburnt Country* (Pl. 36)

Detail *Postscript to the Dreaming* (Pl. 97)

Detail *A Tribute to Caroline Chisholm* (Pl. 67)

Australia's isolation has freed many from the constraints of tradition and encouraged experimentation. Articles which began to appear in the craft journals in the mid '80s attest to a period of vigorous growth (Cooper and Outteridge, 1984, 1985; Gero and Holland, 1986). Some, like Janice Irvine (Antmann, 1985), were extending the craft beyond patchwork, to use the fabric as a canvas for painting, and the needle as a means of adding texture.

The well-established embroiderers' guilds provided a network for teaching and with the explosion of interest in quiltmaking, quilters' guilds were inaugurated in several states. Guilds serve to promote quiltmaking and act as an information exchange, providing workshops and newsletters like The Quilters' Guild's *Template*.

For many, quilts are an introduction to colour and design, allowing creative exploration within a domestic, non-threatening framework. With confidence, quiltmakers can develop their own distinctive style and pass beyond an initial preoccupation with the number of stitches to the inch, to the visual impact of the work. The considerable time involved in making a quilt is often justified by the feeling for the person the quilt is made for.

In a letter to the Guild, Marjorie Coleman, a leading Western Australian quiltmaker, describes quilts as 'messages from women — often the only voice they have and sometimes without their realising what they are doing'.

DIANNE FINNEGAN
PRESIDENT
THE QUILTERS' GUILD

Detail *Our Patch of Australia*, reverse side (Pl. 62)

Detail *Bankstown* (Pl. 20)

Detail *Sydney Harbour on a Sunday Afternoon* (Pl. 82)

A CELEBRATION IN FABRIC

QUILT AUSTRALIA '88

Detail *Love, Life, Liberty* (Pl. 6)

Quilt Australia '88 is very much a celebration of the art of quiltmaking in Australia from 1788 to the present day. The exhibition has drawn on quilts from every state, and from a highly diverse group of professional and amateur quiltmakers.

Arranged by The Quilters' Guild, with support from the Visual Arts/Craft Board of the Australia Council, this vibrant exhibition brings together an exceptional collection of Australian quilts — past and present, traditional and experimental.

For many quiltmakers the exhibition, and the occasion of Australia's Bicentenary, prompted a new approach — a strongly felt desire to sum up their experiences, to understand, and often rethink, the world around them. The five entry categories for the exhibition were traditional, patriotic, political, personal and natural. These were designed to encourage broad individual interpretation and a variety of approaches, whether traditional, contemporary, abstract or pictorial.

The exhibition quilts speak for themselves. They not only celebrate the medium of fabric and fibre art techniques, but also the vitality and directness so characteristic of Australian quiltmaking.

Australian quiltmakers have inherited an assortment of quilting ideas and techniques from the traditions of England, America, Europe and Asia. It is Australia's geographic isolation from these traditional sources that has encouraged and nurtured the growth of a uniquely Australian quiltmaking tradition.

In many cases, especially for those living in remote outback areas, quiltmakers have had no other choice but to solve creative problems in very individual ways. This has led, quite naturally, to innovative quiltmaking techniques and often startling originality of design. The resulting quilts not only reflect the idiosyncrasies, concerns and ideals of their makers, but are rooted in the pragmatic 'give it a go' philosophy so fundamental to Australian development over the last two hundred years.

While some quiltmakers depict their immediate world of family, home and environment, others prefer to work in a more detached and traditional style, making symmetrical designs in which the quilting stitch is the most important dynamic. For many, the quilt is a satisfying medium for exploring social, cultural and political ideas — *One Fifteenth of 'The Quilt and Sheet Show'* (Pl. 59), *But I Like A Happy Ending* (Pl. 14).

Detail *Impressions of Broken Hill* (Pl. 24)

Many quiltmakers find that their ideas and images only become clear through the process of making the quilt, piece by piece and stitch by stitch. At all stages, the quilt itself can assume a dominant life of its own, and simply 'take over'. A certain idea may become more important, a particular colour can suggest a new direction, or a finished quilt top may need an unexpected type of quilting.

Some quiltmakers are also professional artists working in other mediums such as painting and sculpture. For many of them the medium of fabric offers new challenges, and a means of achieving greater freedom of expression — *Impressions of an Australian Landscape* (Pl. 49), *Pansies* (Pl. 34), *The Six Faces of Australia* (Pl. 76), *Impressions of Broken Hill* (Pl. 24), *Monday, at Work on the Willoughby Bicentennial Banners* (Pl. 61), *Fragment: After the Rain* (Pl. 39), *Silver Fish Quilt* (Pl. 15).

Some of the exhibition quilts were made by groups who worked together at each stage, from conception through to the finished quilt. These groups were made up of all kinds of people from school children to professionals. All involved found the creative collaboration rewarding and gained a special sense of community. This feeling was reinforced by the central theme of the Bicentenary — *Dubbo Bicentennial Quilt* (Pl. 92), *Windmills Turning the Past into the Future* (Pl. 69), *Our Patch of Australia* (Pl. 62), . . . *And in the Beginning* (Pl. 37), *Our Part of the Country* (Pl. 27), *A Tribute to Caroline Chisholm* (Pl. 67), *Adelaide: The Years Between 1836-1988* (Pl. 19), *National Focus* (Pl. 57), *Nocturne for the Nation's Capital* (Pl. 21), *Landscape — Eternal Summer* (Pl. 42), *Transport 1788-1988* (Pl. 72), *Bicentennial Birds, Beasts and Blossoms* (Pl. 22).

Detail *Our Patch of Australia* (Pl. 62)

The tactile quality of fabric, and the desire to touch a quilt, are important aspects of quiltmaking. The kinds of fabric used determine a quilt's 'personality' or mood as much as the quiltmaker's choice of images, colours and patterns. The more traditional fabrics like cotton, silk and wool can be mixed with less conventional ones like lurex, felt, leather, organza and even waterproof nylon that crackles when touched. Fabric's tactile dimension is extended and developed by stitches, surface embroidery, beading, and often by the addition of 'found' objects, from shoe laces and safety pins to Victorian corsets — *Midnight Garden* (Pl. 3), *Bouquet* (Pl. 33). The quilting stitch can be used, very effectively, to emphasise line, movement and direction — *Cue In, Gondwana* (Pl. 52), . . . *And in the Beginning* (Pl. 37), *Aerodrome* (Pl. 31).

Detail *Bouquet* (Pl. 33)

Detail *Unchanging Hues* (Pl. 79)

Many quilts make use of soft sculpture effects. They may have loosely attached applique, forming sails of yachts, *Sydney Harbour on a Sunday Afternoon* (Pl. 82); and bundled, bunched and padded material creating flowers, gumnuts, *Unchanging Hues* (Pl. 79), and even stalactites, *Caves* (Pl. 73).

Detail *Bicentennial Birds, Beasts and Blossoms* (Pl. 22)

Detail *Cue In, Gondwana* (Pl. 52)

For many quiltmakers the actual process of sewing — the movement of needle and thread on fabric — is the most important part of making a quilt. For some, stitching is a meditative and connective link with both the present and the past. Different stitches can produce very different effects. Tacking threads are occasionally left in, *Woman's Mirror* (Pl. 101); frayed edges and rich, colourful stitching can create a very striking view of the landscape, *Impressions of Broken Hill* (Pl. 24).

Recurring shapes and symbols are an important part of both traditional and more experimental quilts. The repetition of a particular shape in a pattern, for example, a triangle, ultimately gives it a transcending force of its own — *Sail Away* (Pl. 12), *Birds in the Air* (Pl. 11). This symbolic force, although often elusive, is also strongly evident in totemic arrangements and circles.

The repetition of geometric shapes is most powerfully seen in medallion quilts. The medallion design, one of the oldest found in quilts, grows out from the quilt centre and achieves a quintessential symmetry in the balance of its elements — *Love, Life, Liberty* (Pl. 6), *Lone Star Medallion* (Pl. 4).

Experimental and abstract quilt design uses these traditional or archetypal shapes and forms in forceful and authoritative new ways. Geometric forms are used to create optical illusions which clearly underline the relationship between contemporary quiltmaking and modern art — *Reef Series, Into the Shallows* (Pl. 55), *Reef Series, Oil Slick* (Pl. 56), *The Red Centre* (Pl. 45), *Opals* (Pl. 102), *Journey To* (Pl. 83).

The modern quilt, like modern art, represents a fusion of many diverse influences

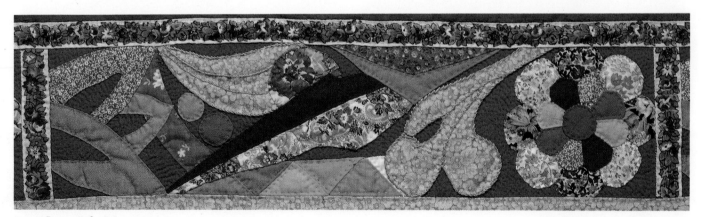

Detail *Love, Life, Liberty* (Pl. 6)

Detail *Australian Genesis* (Pl. 30)

Some quiltmakers use the landscape motif as a starting point, then make a 'leap' from the pictorial to a more abstract and personal interpretation — *Australian Opal* (Pl. 46), *Rock Quilt* (Pl. 50).

Detail *Landscapes* (Pl. 40)

and ideas, and often moves beyond the purely pictorial to an abstract design of real significance — *Breaking of the Drought* (Pl. 88), *Peninsula* (Pl. 5), *Dullflower No. 5 . . . The Orchid* (Pl. 26), *Fragment: After the Rain* (Pl. 39), *National Focus* (Pl. 57), *Coal Mine Quilt — A Personal Record* (Pl. 58).

Although most Australians live along the seaboard, the interior landscape is, for many, the heartland of Australia. The outback landscape, rather than urban life, has become a powerhouse of both personal and universal symbols for quiltmakers.

The landscape is used in several ways. Some quilts capture pictorial qualities; the subject may be animals, *Australian Genesis* (Pl. 30); a flower, *Unchanging Hues* (Pl. 79), *Wild Flower Study: Leschenaultia biloba* (Pl. 8); a place, *Our Part of the Country* (Pl. 27); or even a particular building, *Rainbow Serpent at the Opera House* (Pl. 32).

Detail *Landscapes* (Pl. 40)

21

Detail *Impressions of Broken Hill* (Pl. 24)

The landscape is traditionally imbued with qualities of endurance and timelessness. Many quiltmakers have tried to convey these qualities by incorporating historical elements, people, places and events into their designs — *Old Houses of Australia* (Pl. 7), *Bankstown* (Pl. 20), *A Tribute to Caroline Chisholm* (Pl. 67), *Adelaide: The Years Between 1836-1988* (Pl. 19), *Transport 1788-1988* (Pl. 72), *Impressions of Broken Hill* (Pl. 24), *Two Hundred Years of Australian History* (Pl. 86).

The Bicentenary has inspired some quiltmakers to explore the theme of the Aborigines' place in Australian history, culture and ethos, and to include Aboriginal art motifs and techniques in their own work — *Tribute to the Dreamtime* (Pl. 29), *Dreamtime — Land and Sea* (Pl. 91), *Rainbow Serpent* (Pl. 53), *Rainbow Serpent at the Opera House* (Pl. 32). *Australian Genesis* (Pl. 30) makes bold use of the strong images and colours typical of Aboriginal art.

Colour represents a special challenge for the Australian quiltmaker. Often a quilt's colour scheme depends a great deal on the individual's perception of light. Some quiltmakers perceive Australian colours as hard, brash and bright, while others perceive and interpret them as a subtle range of tones — *Landscapes* (Pl. 40), *The Red Centre* (Pl. 45).

Many quiltmakers try to achieve a balance of hard and soft colours. In an effort to show the strength and clarity of Australian light, some have sought to find exactly the right colours, *Nandalie* (Pl. 104), tones and textures of fabric. In *Spirit of Australia* (Pl. 87) quality of light is conveyed by the image of a blazing sun which dominates the design.

An advertisement of 1834
encouraging young women to emigrate

Detail *A Tribute to Caroline Chisholm* (Pl. 67)

The movement of quilts from bed to wall signified a general recognition of quilts as art objects. This recognition gave quiltmakers far more artistic licence to experiment — quilts no longer had to be washable, or a particular size or shape, or restricted to traditional fabrics. Quilts were no longer *just* bedspreads. This new freedom meant that quilts could be treated like sculptured objects, to be studied and walked around and through, *Hanging Red Gum Leaves* (Pl. 66). In this case the shape of the quilt relates very directly to the design, and is an extension of it. The shape of a quilt can be irregular, *Pansies* (Pl. 34), *Past, Present and Future* (Pl. 85); or consist of more than one part, *Reef Series, Into the Shallows* (Pl. 55).

Detail *The Red Centre* (Pl. 45)

Detail *Two Hundred Years of Australian History* (Pl. 86)

Australian quiltmakers are renowned for their determination, innovation and a certain brash confidence in the intrinsic value of their work. In this bicentennial year, they are proud inheritors of an Australian craft tradition reaching back two hundred years; a legacy of artistic achievements rich in historic and cultural associations.

Quilt Australia '88 is positive proof that today's quiltmakers are aware, confident and adventurous. They demonstrate a facility to explore, experiment, improvise and create, beyond the known limits. This lively approach to the art of quiltmaking is, in itself, Australia's guarantee of further achievements.

ALISON HALLIDAY

Plate 3 *Midnight Garden* Mary Hinde, Sydney, NSW
DESCRIPTION: 240 × 110 cm; cotton, mixtures; beaded, quilted

It is a continuation of my love of scrap quilts. I began to cut and sew and modified my ideas along the way. The decorative and visual impact is of prime importance to me.

Plate 4 *Lone Star Medallion* Val Nadin, Sydney, NSW
DESCRIPTION: 268 × 180 cm; cotton; machine and hand pieced, hand applique and quilted

I believe very strongly in the old adage that 'a quilt is not a quilt until it is quilted' and always achieve greater satisfaction doing elaborate quilting than I do from the piecing.

Plate 5 *Peninsula* Pamela Timmins, Sydney, NSW
DESCRIPTION: 150 × 150 cm; cotton, some tea-dyed; applique, embroidered, quilted

The starting point for me was a collection of photographs and a very old house which until recently, had been a family weekend retreat. I would like the quilt to be regarded as a naive painting, in fabric instead of paint.

Plate 6 *Love, Life, Liberty* Jennifer Lewis, Melbourne, Vic
DESCRIPTION: 200 × 200 cm; cotton; pieced applique, reverse applique, embroidered, quilted

The inspiration was the plaster ceiling of the bedroom in our family home where our family grew up and where we endeavoured to equip them for life with a security and love of family closeness, yet the ability to be free and creative people.

Plate 7 *Old Houses of Australia* Narelle Grieve, Sydney, NSW
DESCRIPTION: 134 × 134 cm; synthetic fabric, silk threads; hand quilted and trapunto

Houses fascinate me. I researched in libraries for pictures of old houses. The design shows the assortment of houses built in early Australian times, some very English and totally unsuited to Australian conditions. As time went by Australians found their own style in a mixture of both. The centre of the quilt is a ceiling rose plaster decoration and the border design was commonly used in stencilling the interior walls.

Plate 8 *Wild Flower Study: Leschenaultia biloba* Wendy Wycherley, Perth, WA
DESCRIPTION: 118 × 136 cm; hand dyed and painted cotton; hand applique, quilted

The finished quilt, as is the way with finished quilts, does not say 'end of story'. Instead, it says to me 'what if . . .?'

Plate 9 *Picnics Past* Helen Macartney, Sydney, NSW
DESCRIPTION: 147 × 147 cm; cotton and linen tablecloths, teatowels and aprons (both old and new); machine pieced, applique, hand quilted

These fabrics recall the domestic life of my childhood. Their variety and familiarity inspire me and evoke many ideas.

Plate 10 *The Gibson Quilt No. 1* Carol Ireland, New Town, Tas
DESCRIPTION: 188 × 136 cm; calico flour bags; machine pieced, hand quilted

I was not aware when I purchased the first flour bag at a market stall that my family was in any way related to the Gibsons. The design on the lower central bag was made by my uncle, Jack Read, when he was a boy. He is now aged 83 years. One bonus point, arising from this work: while sewing the bags, I became aware of a faint, but unmistakable odour of flour, which accompanied me throughout the project.

Plate 11 *Birds in the Air* Georgina Child, Colorado, USA
DESCRIPTION: 200 × 200 cm; cotton; hand pieced and quilted

I didn't really have a good idea of what it would look like when I started. It just grew as each block was finished. This quilt has been five years in the making, travelling to England, Scotland, California and Colorado and back and forth several times to Australia!

Plate 12 *Sail Away* Diana Goulston Robinson, New York, USA
DESCRIPTION: 230 × 178 cm; cotton; machine and hand pieced, hand quilted

My quilt is made up of many small scraps (961 different fabrics); the stuff of people's lives.
The many varied pieces are cut to the same size and shape, but, like people, they are different
prints, textures and colours. Like Australia, the quilt contains a diversity of 'personalities',
accumulated and adapted to an integrated balanced whole.

Plate 13 *Memories of Saturday Afternoons* Judy Hooworth, Sydney, NSW
DESCRIPTION: 200 × 226 cm; cotton, blends; machine pieced, hand applique, machine and hand quilted

Because I live on the coast being an Australian means being aware of the beach and the suburbs. Saturday afternoons are lazy, often sunny, a time to relax and visit with friends and family. I've tried to interpret this feeling in my quilt, it's relaxed and unhurried. I can't imagine life without a quilt in progress.

Plate 14 *But I Like A Happy Ending* Sue Rowley, Wollongong, NSW
DESCRIPTION: 200 × 172 cm; screen printed cotton, polycotton; machine pieced, hand quilted

My quilt is about 'splitting up'. There is no free space in the home depicted here — it cannot accommodate change in the woman, who is leaving, suitcase in hand. This quilt also recalls and celebrates domestic space and relationships with a sense of nostalgia.

Plate 15 *Silver Fish Quilt* Jane Mitchell, East Fremantle, WA
DESCRIPTION: 156 × 112 cm; hand painted cotton, synthetics; machine pieced, embroidered, quilted

I often choose a theme or image which I then work through and portray using a variety of different media and techniques. I approach my painting on fabric in almost the same way as when painting on paper or canvas. Quilting and embroidery then add new dimensions to the qualities of the paintings.

36

Plate 16 *Oz Icon* Wendy Holland, Sydney, NSW
DESCRIPTION: 243 × 183 cm; old and new cotton; machine pieced, hand quilted

I tried to combine brash Australian ugliness with an underlying breadth of landscape and a
sense of the timeless Aboriginal totem. Hopefully the end result is more than the sum of its
parts. The fabrics 'took over' more than I expected.

Plate 17 *Journey Through Life* Sandy Ward, Melbourne, Vic
DESCRIPTION: 150 × 210 cm; painted and dyed cotton, polycotton; machine pieced, machine and hand quilted

It is a breakthrough, in as much as my previous work has followed a repeating block format, while this quilt is non-repeating and is based on an attempt to convey a journey through various stages of life using some of the symbolic meanings of colours.

Plate 18 *Childhood Memories* Trudy Billingsley, Sydney, NSW
DESCRIPTION: 180 × 244 cm; silk, satin, lurex, organza, cotton; machine pieced, hand dyed and quilted

As a child I lived for many years near a lighthouse at the mouth of the Shoalhaven River on the south coast. It was important to me in this quilt to show the significance of the light. Quilting has been used to give dimension, movement and direction to the sea hitting the rocks and the light's strength as it pierces the night sky.

Plate 19 *Adelaide: The Years Between 1836-1988* The Quilters' Guild of South Australia, Adelaide, SA
DESCRIPTION: 170 × 122 cm; cotton, polycotton, lawn, silk, satin, lace; pictorial applique, hand quilted

The Quilters' Guild of South Australia has not previously attempted a pictorial quilt, and in doing so, a sense of creativity and achievement was established between fellow quilters who worked together on the project.

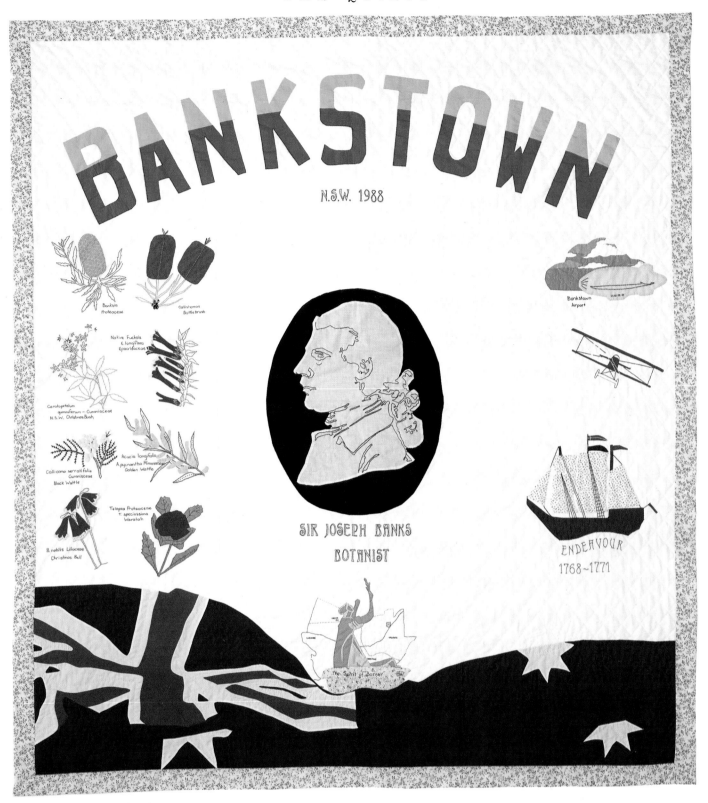

Plate 20 *Bankstown* Barbara Radzevicius, Sydney, NSW
DESCRIPTION: 240 × 222 cm; cotton; applique, embroidered, quilted

I love the city of Bankstown, especially the beautiful flora native to this area. My central medallion of Joseph Banks, portrayed facing native flora, was the starting point. At the bottom a statue called 'Spirit of Botany' is wrapped in the beautiful, blue flag. The colours are everything.

Plate 21 *Nocturne for the Nation's Capital* Canberra Bluebell Quilters, Canberra, ACT
DESCRIPTION: 120 × 120 cm; silk, polyester, rayon; machine and hand pieced, applique, tied

Living in Canberra, we all appreciate the beauty of our capital city, and wanted to express this in a quilt. Each member chose a Canberra landmark to feature in her block, which she designed herself, and then added applique and embroidery for the detail.

Plate 22 *Bicentennial Birds, Beasts and Blossoms* Star of the Sea College, Melbourne, Vic
DESCRIPTION: 174 × 141 cm; cotton; painted, embroidered, quilted

This quilt is a 'first' by a group of junior students aged twelve and thirteen. We represented characters and animals from Australian literature past and present. We feel that quiltmaking brought us together in a special way.

Plate 23 *The Founding of Australia* Jan Frazer, Melbourne, Vic
DESCRIPTION: 100 × 130 cm; hand dyed and painted cotton; machine pieced and quilted

My original idea was to reproduce, as faithfully as I could, the Talmage painting, *The Founding of Australia* (the landing of Captain Phillip). I found that the use of fabrics gave an alternative and perhaps starker view of the scene than the available print of the painting.

Plate 24 *Impressions of Broken Hill* Margaret Maccioni, Sydney, NSW
DESCRIPTION: 135 × 112 cm; mixed fabrics; machine applique, hand embroidered and quilted

I enjoy the challenge of interpreting my feelings and impressions through the colour and texture of fabrics. It's a kind of metamorphosis — fabric becomes a tree, for instance, or looking at a tree I can see certain fabrics.

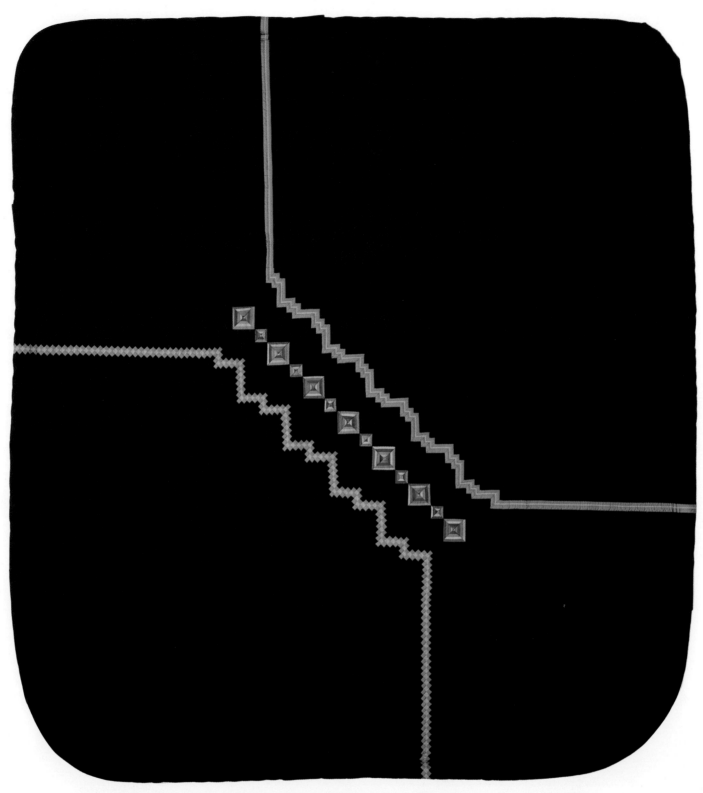

Plate 25 *Fantasy Impromptu* Linda Stern, Melbourne, Vic
DESCRIPTION: 200 × 200 cm; cotton, cotton blends; machine pieced and quilted

Over the last two years I have found that my approach to science and my approach to quilting have become closer to each other. Both science and quiltmaking require a lot of precision work and a lot of perseverance. This quilt was my first experiment in using bright colours and in working directly with the fabric rather than planning ahead.

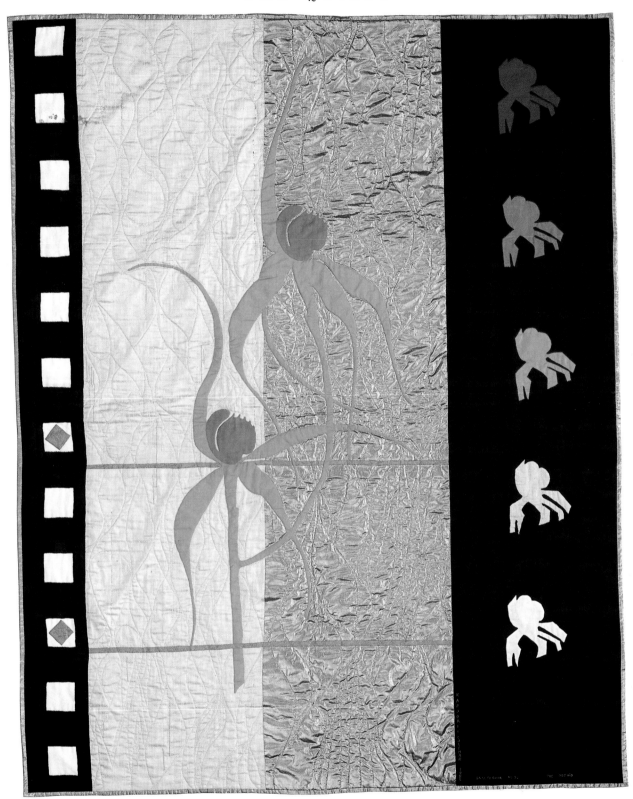

Plate 26 *Dullflower No. 5 . . . The Orchid* Marjorie Coleman, Perth, WA
DESCRIPTION: 185 × 150 cm; silk, cotton, lurex, brocade; machine pieced, hand applique, embroidered and quilted

The word 'dullflower' is ironic. I wanted to suggest a simplicity which conceals a great deal of complication, and delicacy which conceals toughness. Spider orchids are at once very low key, 'shy' and opulent. I saw in this apparent contradiction an analogy to a Japanese screen; formal, stylised, rich and complex.

47

Plate 27 *Our Part of the Country* Wagga Wagga Quilters Group, Wagga Wagga, NSW
DESCRIPTION: 145 × 210 cm; cotton, blends, wool, felt, leather, astrakhan; machine and hand pieced, hand applique, embroidered and quilted

This quilt is definitely a breakthrough for our group as it is the first quilt we have done together. We all put in our ideas at the planning stage and the completed quilt incorporates these ideas in colour and texture. The borders represent Wagga Wagga's colours: gold for finance, prosperity and wheat; green for agriculture and black for industry and the black crow. Wagga Wagga means 'place of many crows'.

Plate 28 *Down Memory Lane* Edith Higgins, Bullaburra, NSW
DESCRIPTION: 164 × 110 cm; mixed fabrics, ribbons, lace; embroidered

I always had in mind to use the leftover scraps from sewing for the family as documentation of having 'been there'. The starting point was a 'crazy patchwork' workshop and realising that here was the answer to using up my collection. Crazy patchwork is associated with bygone years and I wanted to underline that impression.

Plate 29 *Tribute to the Dreamtime* Lucy Hill, Caloundra, Qld
DESCRIPTION: 151 × 110 cm; cotton, polycotton; machine pieced, hand applique, embroidered and quilted

I was particularly impressed by the X-ray bark paintings from the Western Arnhem Land area, especially the work of Yirawala and Bobby Barrdjaray Nganjmira. I wanted to convey in fabric my admiration for the work of a great artist from a different culture.

Plate 30 *Australian Genesis* Jennie Stevens, Canberra, ACT
DESCRIPTION: 165 × 107 cm; hand dyed and painted fabrics; reverse applique, hand quilted

Quiltmaking is a unique art form which uses the colour, pattern and texture of fabrics, with the added dimensional effect of quilting. This quilt is an expression of my admiration for the Australian Aborigines and their inherent and pervasive spirituality, seen especially in their bark and rock paintings.

Plate 31 *Aerodrome* Jan Irvine, Sydney, NSW
DESCRIPTION: 120 × 250 cm; air brush dyed silk; hand quilted

The light in the Australian landscape is, at times, arresting and timelessly beautiful.

Plate 32 *Rainbow Serpent at the Opera House* Helen Slocombe, Sydney, NSW
DESCRIPTION: 200 × 168 cm; cotton, polycotton; machine pieced, hand quilted and applique

Quiltmaking has influenced the way I look at everything from nature to architecture. Colour is all important in this quilt and had to portray the excitement of Australia and the clarity of its light. I've always been fascinated with Aboriginal art and wished to produce their spontaneous animal images. I almost felt as if the fabrics had manipulated me into producing the quilt, and then the title was born.

Plate 33 *Bouquet* Lois Densham, Melbourne, Vic
DESCRIPTION: 150 × 150 cm; recycled embroidered table cloths, ribbons, cotton, voile; machine applique, hand quilted

By using recycled fabrics with another identity I chose to bring the world into the work. I wanted to use flowers in a happy, joyful way.

Plate 34 *Pansies* Yvonne Chapman, Valley Heights, NSW
DESCRIPTION: 182 × 120 cm; cotton, wool, silk, cotton and wool fibres; machine and hand pieced, embroidered applique, beaded, quilted

I have always loved pansies, especially the purple ones. Colour, to me, always comes first — the rest just flows on: cutting out the basic shapes, using fibres as contour, the extra fabrics and stitching and embroidery for texture. Colours and fabrics flow easily into one another.

Plate 35 *Terania Rainforest* Irma Chelsworth, The Channon via Lismore, NSW
DESCRIPTION: 254 × 192 cm; cotton; machine pieced, hand quilted and applique

This quilt, in its central scene, represents the Terania Rainforest of New South Wales. Rainforest preservation is an urgent issue and the most important idea behind the quilt. The specific inspiration was the scene from my window and the need to express it in fabric. A strong message is contained in the circular quilting pattern of the sawcuts eating into the rainforest, with the background quilting grids raising the motifs into relief.

Plate 36 *A Sunburnt Country* Judy Turner, Canberra, ACT
DESCRIPTION: 140 × 108 cm; cotton, polycotton; machine pieced, hand applique and quilted

This quilt is a continuation of my past efforts to blend printed fabrics, but with a conscious desire to use more colour. The use of colour is the most important part. It's supposed to be like looking at our bush through an octoscope with the colours of the earth and sky blending together.

57

Plate 37 . . . *And in the Beginning* Peel Cottage Quilters, Tamworth, NSW
DESCRIPTION: 125 × 205 cm; cotton, silk; piecework, applique, quilted

Until this time, all fourteen of the Peel Cottage quilters had only worked on traditional quilts. We wanted to make a quilt depicting our familiar rural scene as it would have been 'in the beginning'. Quiltmaking brings us together for companionship, creativity and encouragement.

Plate 38 *200 Flags* Alison Muir, Sydney, NSW
DESCRIPTION: 280 × 280 cm; painted cotton, polycotton; machine pieced and quilted, applique

As my career as an interior designer has progressed into management, my quilt designs have become more important as an expression of my need to design. This collection of flags represents to me, the countries, companies and events which have influenced Australia and Australians over two hundred years.

59

Plate 39 *Fragment: After the Rain* Wendy Lugg, Perth, WA
DESCRIPTION: 122 × 144 cm; hand printed and painted cotton, polyester; machine pieced, hand applique, quilted and embroidered

Painting satisfied my love of colour, but not my desire to achieve a deeper surface to my pictures. I work in a variety of textile techniques, particularly printing and dyeing, and do not see each as a separate activity. This quilt is the second in a series of quilts, each celebrating a small fragment of the vast Australian expanses.

Plate 40 *Landscapes* Beverley Sach, Canberra, ACT
DESCRIPTION: 250 × 200 cm; polycotton; machine pieced, hand and machine applique, embroidered, quilted

This quilt is entirely pictorial in a stylised way; it went beyond my original conception and developed a life of its own as it was made.

61

Plate 41 *Meditation in Motion* Jill Vanderkooi, Blaxland, NSW
DESCRIPTION: 100 × 115 cm; cotton; hand pieced and quilted

This quilt is my first original design. I was inspired when I saw Kinetic Dance Company perform in a garden at a gallery. I have tried to create a feeling of distance, tranquillity, colour and movement.

Plate 42 *Landscape — Eternal Summer* Batik Association of ACT , Canberra, ACT
DESCRIPTION: 300 × 230 cm; drimarene dyes on twill silk; machine pieced, hand embroidered and quilted

The beginning and the final solution was the first 'doodle'. Everyone involved was asked to draw their favourite shape; the shape that keeps recurring in their work and is part of their overall design concept.

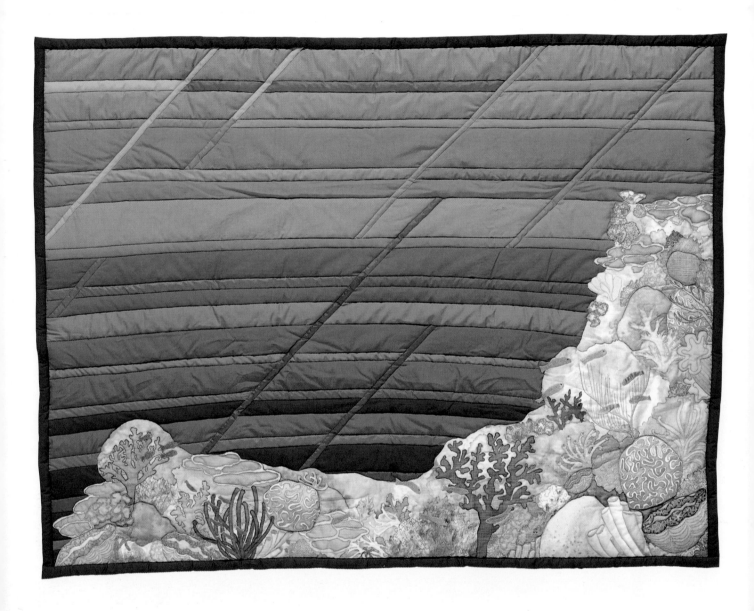

Plate 43 *Barrier Reef Quilt (2)* Cynthia Morgan, Brisbane, Qld
DESCRIPTION: 105 × 135 cm; cotton, silk, polyester; hand dyed, painted, machine and hand embroidered, hand
quilted

I have used the varied colours of live coral, sea anemones and other sea creatures. Hand
quilted lines imply movement and machine quilting and embroidery have been used to enhance
the coral forms.

Plate 44 *Emma's Quilt* Sally Evers (designer) and Betty Brown (maker), Kettering, Tas
DESCRIPTION: 234 × 234 cm; cotton, polyester; machine pieced, hand quilted Photography by Uffe Schulze

This quilt was made for Margaret (Emma) Mathews. Many of the fabrics used in it are cut from Emma's old clothes. Her preference is for very bright colours, particularly reds and greens. The challenge was to tone down the high-key colours, without them losing their vibrancy, to make a bed quilt suitable for Emma's small country cottage. The overlay of large triangular grids which dissect the triangles help to harmonise the total design, yet accent the large number of different fabrics used.

65

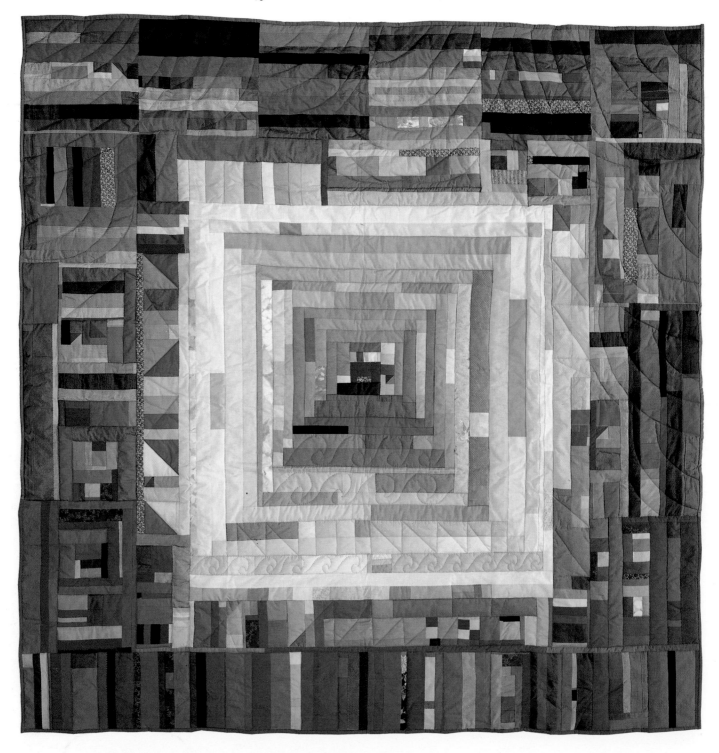

Plate 45 *The Red Centre* Joy Woodgate, Sydney, NSW
DESCRIPTION: 175 × 175 cm; cotton, polycotton; strip pieced, machine quilted

There is a tradition of patchwork in my family. My great-grandmother migrated to Australia with her family in 1906 from South Africa. Unfortunately the only piece of 'patchy patchy' of hers that remains is a cushion cover. My great Aunt Jessie made us all pinwheel quilts — maybe about 50. They both used every scrap of fabric. I feel my quilt is very much a part of them. When I think of Australia I think of the blue haze, the desert, the red centre, the beaches and ocean.

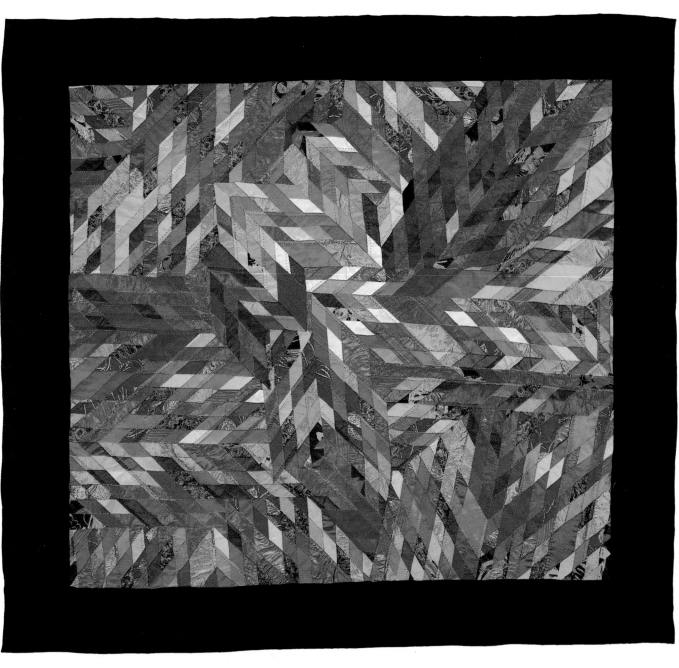

Plate 46 *Australian Opal* Diana Thomas, Sydney, NSW
DESCRIPTION: 134 × 146 cm; polyester, taffeta, silk, lame, satin; English hand piecing technique

My father used to tell me of my grandfather, a wool classer, who brought rocks full of opal back to Sydney which were then used as door stops in their house. The brooch, which gave me the idea for the wall hanging, belonged to my great-grandmother who lived in Tasmania. I wanted the wall hanging to flash as the light hit it so I've used fabrics which reflect light readily.

Plate 47 *Building Blocks* Karen Fail, Sydney, NSW
DESCRIPTION: 200 × 170 cm; cotton, polycotton, lame; machine pieced, hand quilted

This is a personal statement of the way a church family functions. The idea 'every piece is important' is central to the design of the quilt and is reflected in the use of many different shapes and sizes. Purple and gold are colours traditionally associated with the church.

Plate 48 *Mousetrap* Felicity Naess, Hazelbrook, NSW
DESCRIPTION: 148 × 116 cm; cotton; hand and machine pieced, hand quilted

I wanted a contemporary, lively feeling using a traditional pattern. I always admired the movement of the 'Snail Trail' pattern and wanted to play with this to create a quilt where the pattern's natural movement was supported by colour choice, toning and change in pattern size. At the back of my mind was a picture of green leaves and pink and purple flowers.

Plate 49 *Impressions of an Australian Landscape* Jenny Martyn, Melbourne, Vic
DESCRIPTION: 200 × 150 cm; cotton, silk, leather, found objects; hand and machine pieced, applique, quilted, stuffed

I never design or plan on paper. Any work I have planned in detail has been an unmitigated disaster. Instead I plan in my mind and visualise how I will use fabrics to achieve the textures and ideas I wish to project. The decorative and visual aspects of my quilts are the most important — what you see is what you get!

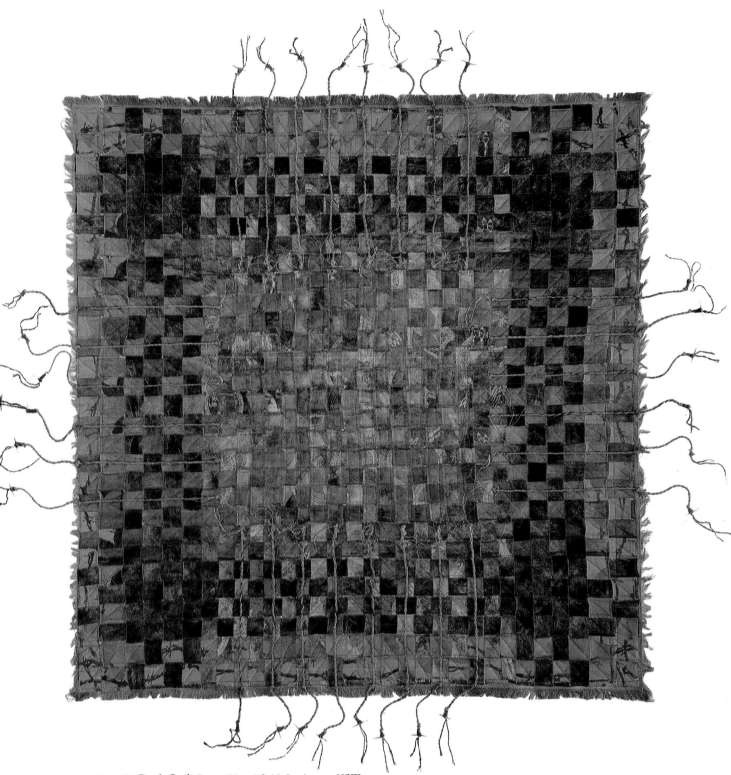

Plate 50 *Rock Quilt* Susan Blanchfield, Jamberoo, NSW
DESCRIPTION: 181 × 170 cm; silk, hand printed cotton, human hair handspun by Peter Blacksmith, quills

The Australian landscape is the source for all my work. I am concerned about the fragmentation of what was once whole, of the imposition of geometric order on organic order. The quilt's design motifs are the kangaroo, taken from the dollar note; the emu, taken from an Aboriginal art book; and the leaves from the brush box tree.

Plate 51 *Mandala* Greg Somerville, Lawson, NSW
DESCRIPTION: 100 × 159 cm; cotton painted with fabric dyes; hand quilted

The concept of an intricate network of things and patterns relating across many levels is hinted at in this design. The mandala can represent one individual or societies of individuals, and how the artist views these entities. Mandalas are both personal and spiritual.

Plate 52 *Cue In, Gondwana* Marjorie Coleman, Perth, WA
DESCRIPTION: 198 × 180 cm; cotton, rayon, polyester; machine pieced, hand applique and quilted

This quilt is more of an 'ideas' piece in which the decorative aspects are less important. It is narrative. Applique, piecing and quilting tell a story. For years I have heard about Gondwana, a southern hemisphere super-continent, which broke up piece by piece beginning about 200 million years ago, with the pieces becoming our familiar southern continents. I do not normally use Aboriginal symbols and patterns, but the pattern is that of a message stick given to my father by nomadic Aborigines, as a sort of passport, when he led a survey expedition in 1932, retracing John Forrest's earlier journey across Western Australia.

Plate 53 *Rainbow Serpent* Karen Allison, Devonport, Tas
DESCRIPTION: 140 × 120 cm; hand painted polycotton; hand quilted

From start to finish the original idea has never changed. I have tried to make a statement about Aboriginal culture. I felt so strongly about the theme that I realised it was not just an idea, but a statement about my heritage that I had to make.

Plate 54 *All that Jizz* Pamela Tawton, Canberra, ACT
DESCRIPTION: 190 × 140 cm; cotton, polycotton; 'stained glass' technique, embroidered, quilted

My initial research was aided by access to a fine library of bird books owned by my employer, Dr. Alan Cowan. It was most important that I had the birds' colour and environment just right.

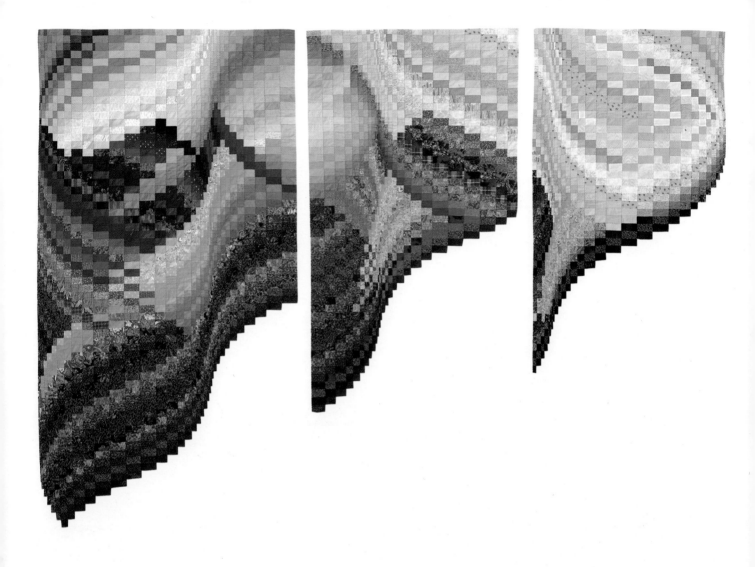

Plate 55 *Reef Series, Into the Shallows* Susan Denton, Melbourne, Vic
DESCRIPTION: 270 × 370 cm; cotton, polyester batting; machine pieced and quilted

This triptych is the ninth and final piece of work in the 'Reef Series', which has occupied a large part of my life for two years. It is a celebration of the colours, complexity and fragility of the Great Barrier Reef. Colour foremost and pattern secondly are the two aspects which have continually preoccupied me. Quiltmaking is the way I express what I feel and think.

Plate 56 *Reef Series, Oil Slick* Susan Denton, Melbourne, Vic
DESCRIPTION: 180 × 180 cm; cotton, polyester batting; machine pieced and quilted Photography by Photohouse Graphics

The sweep of the lines of colour is intended to convey the clogging results of oil on coral and in water. I don't regard this quilt as decorative, but as an angry piece of work. The lines are intended to be visually forceful and threatening.

Plate 57 *National Focus* Fibre Five, Canberra, ACT
DESCRIPTION: 220 × 160 cm; hand dyed cotton, polycotton; applique, machine pieced and quilted

Our previous quilts were collaborative efforts, each member went off and completed her
section and then the pieces were joined. This quilt is quite different in that the progress has
been extremely slow, requiring consensus for each design stage. The finished image evolved
over a period of 18 months, capturing the approach of the Bicentenary. Our quilt reflects this
by focusing on the new national Parliament House as it emerged from the landscape.

Plate 58 *Coal Mine Quilt — A Personal Record* Perry McIntyre, Sydney, NSW
DESCRIPTION: 185 × 185 cm; mixed fabrics; machine pieced, hand quilted

The self-expression possible in this type of quilt is terrifically stimulating. If I didn't like the look, I cut it off! I wanted a pictorial quilt to somehow convey the coal, the mines in general, the evolution of the coal, and the stark isolation that is often felt in these towns, as well as the good times and the beauty.

Plate 59 *One Fifteenth of 'The Quilt and Sheet Show'* Lorraine Hepburn, Sydney, NSW
DESCRIPTION: 170 × 190 cm; polycotton painted with fabric ink; machine stitched

I work as a full-time sculptor. I wanted to say something humorous. This quilt is one fifteenth of a sculptural installation about communication between men and women, which featured in 'The Quilt and Sheet Show'.

Plate 60 *Hello Australia* Yolanda Gifford, Sydney, NSW
DESCRIPTION: 195 × 137 cm; cotton, satin binding; machine and hand pieced, applique, quilted

One day I remembered a Sydney drawing office I used to work in where there were seventeen members of staff. Sixteen were different nationalities and only one was born in Australia. I am a mixture, like my quilt. I was born in New Guinea but have lived in Australia most of my life. I am a sixth generation Australian on my mother's side, and my father was born in Belgium.

81

Plate 61 *Monday, at Work on the Willoughby Bicentennial Banners* Margaret Maccioni, Sydney, NSW
DESCRIPTION: 120 × 147 cm; mixed fabrics; machine applique, hand embroidered and quilted

For week after week I sat at the same spot and the image of the room and the women at work, became fixed in my mind. This is a tribute to Yvonne Line and her helpers in that huge project, and to the interest it has generated in the community.

Plate 62 *Our Patch of Australia* Pimpama Patchworkers, Pimpama, Qld
DESCRIPTION: 214 × 176 cm; cotton, polycotton, hessian, lace, silk, felt; machine and hand applique, embroidered, painted, beaded, trapunto, quilted

This quilt was only the second worked on by the group. We invited many locals and historians to a morning tea and discussed much of the past; then each person researched her own block. We wanted our quilt to reflect the history of the area and our own personal relationships with it.

Plate 63 *Australia Fair* Sally Astridge, Sydney, NSW
DESCRIPTION: 217 × 144 cm; cotton, polycotton; applique, embroidered, quilted

This quilt is to be used on a bed! It stores many happy memories, family occasions and the thrill of Australian wildlife.

Plate 64 *Where Flying Geese Gather* Laurell Brown, Launceston, Tas
DESCRIPTION: 265 × 204 cm; cotton; pieced, applique, embroidered, quilted

This is the story of my family's history. My family came from many different parts of Europe, migrating to a new land. To me, a quilt is an expression of the relationship between the maker and the recipient and provides comfort and memory.

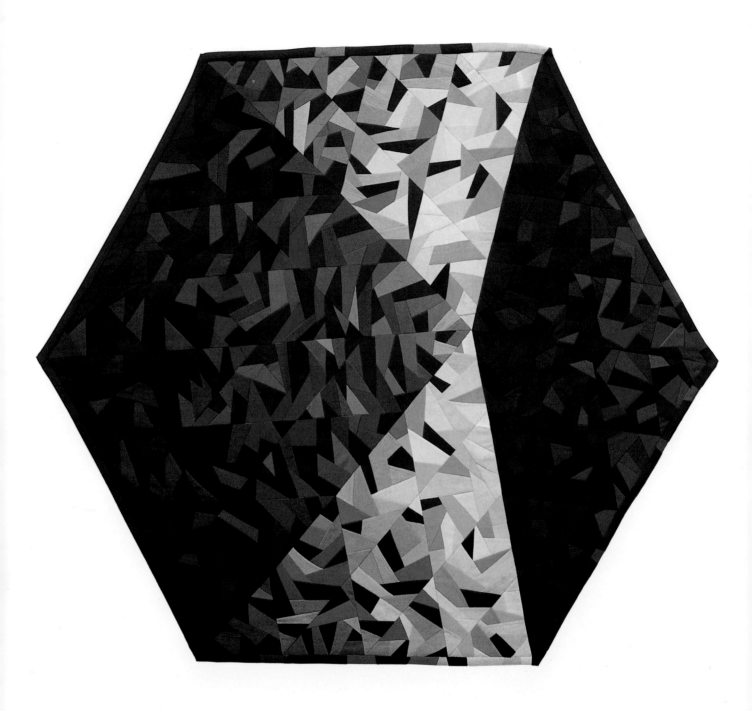

Plate 65 *Crazy Hexagon* Barbara Macey, Melbourne, Vic
DESCRIPTION: 158 × 180 cm; wool, wool and synthetic blends; machine pieced using the 'sew and fold' technique
Photography by Photohouse Graphics

The visual aspect is the most important part of the design. I wanted the light and dark areas
to stand out in strong contrast, suggesting an ambiguous, slightly three-dimensional space.
There is no quilting or other surface decoration because I wanted to make *Crazy Hexagon*
uncompromisingly contemporary and personal yet clearly a descendant of old crazy quilts.

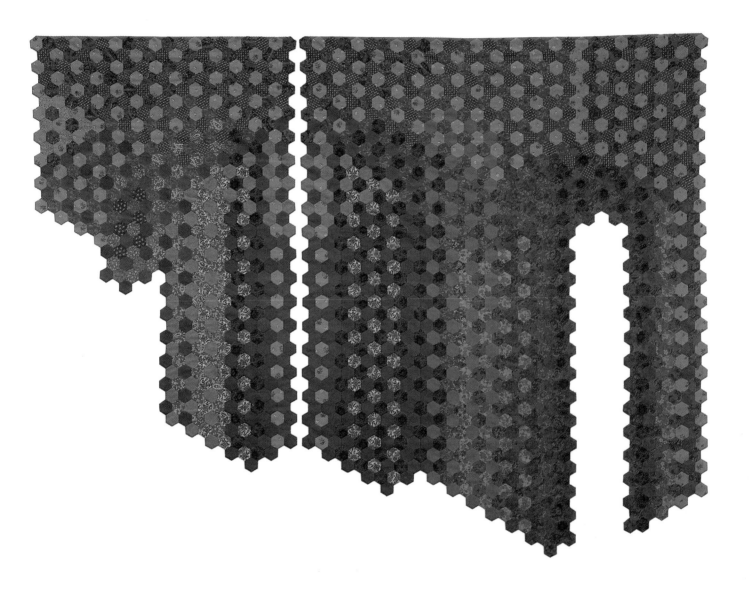

Plate 66 *Hanging Red Gum Leaves* Nancy Tingey, Canberra, ACT
DESCRIPTION: 171 × 230 cm; wool/cotton (Viyella); English piecing technique

This quilt moves towards open forms using the hexagon as a leaf-like element and building up the overall mass from within, representing growth patterns. I would like the viewer to relate physically to my work, to walk through it and among it, rather as one does among the trees and other natural surroundings.

Plate 67 *A Tribute to Caroline Chisholm* Students of Year 7 (1987), Caroline Chisholm High School, Canberra, ACT
DESCRIPTION: 240 × 180 cm; cotton; machine pieced, silkscreened, hand quilted

The pictures are the students' view of the achievements, events and life of Caroline Chisholm. The patchwork houses and schoolhouse blocks signify the shelter that Caroline Chisholm provided for young women and later for families. The 'flying geese' border is a traditional border pattern representing the migration of settlers to this country.

Plate 68 *Colonial Stars* Ann Haddad, Canberra, ACT
DESCRIPTION: 276 × 230 cm; cotton; machine and hand pieced, hand quilted

Curzon Hall, built in the 1890s, in North Ryde, is very near my parents' home in Sydney. The building has recently been restored and has superb tile flooring. I was interested in preserving the pattern of the tiles and wanted to show the creative possibilities in our history for quiltmakers.

Plate 69 *Windmills Turning the Past into the Future* American Women of Sydney, Sydney, NSW
DESCRIPTION: 255 × 220 cm; cotton, blends; hand pieced, applique, embroidered, hand quilted

Our common bond was an affection for Australia and its culture, and a wish to express this in a form we all enjoy — quilting. The medallion of a sheep station represents Australia yesterday, today and tomorrow; the day-time map of Australia and the night-time map of the USA indicates the vast distances between us. We felt that the motion of the windmill was an important one, thus the gradual colour change in the patchwork blocks around the centre medallion, indicating movement as well as time change.

Plate 70 *High Wall — Open Cut Mine* Christine Ling, Blackwater, Qld
DESCRIPTION: 150 × 150 cm; cotton, polycotton; machine pieced, hand quilted

Although a mine can be an ugly environment the operation actually uncovers the beauty hidden below the earth's surface.

91

Plate 71 *Yankalilla Community Quilt* The Yankalilla Quilting Community, SA
DESCRIPTION: 233 × 195 cm; cotton; pieced, applique, quilted

Yankalilla is about 50 kilometres south of Adelaide, set in a beautiful valley which opens to the sea. In winter the surrounding hills form a patchwork of green and brown hues, in summer they are bleached blonde. This quilt is the effort of about thirty-five local quilters and shows our pride and appreciation of our historical past.

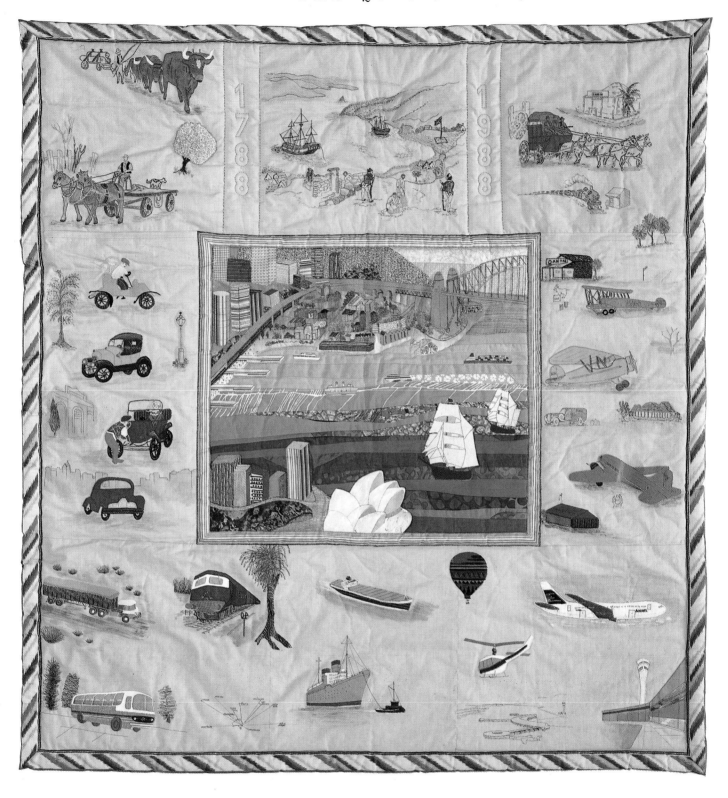

Plate 72 *Transport 1788-1988* Indooroopilly Quilters, Brisbane, Qld
DESCRIPTION: 133 × 120 cm; painted cotton, polycotton; machine pieced, machine and hand embroidered and quilted

Because of the vastness and remoteness of Australia, means of transport have been vital from the very beginning. The use of colour is very important in this quilt. The main background is an earthy colour framed by the sea and coral reefs.

Plate 73 *Caves* Yvonne Line, Sydney, NSW
DESCRIPTION: 180 × 140 cm; taffeta, habutae, cotton twill; machine applique, hand quilted

Quilts are for pleasure as well as for use. As soon as I started on this theme I realised that one quilt would not satisfy all the ideas I have on the subject. Colour is important for impact and interest. The use of different tonings in my applique stitch gives added depth to the work.

Plate 74 *Impressions of Monet* Kerry Beaumont, Hazelbrook, NSW
DESCRIPTION: 117 × 113 cm; Thai silk, satin; machine pieced, hand applique, machine and hand quilted

Quilting is a medium of artistic self-expression which totally absorbs me and fulfills most of my creative needs. This quilt was my first attempt to break with traditional quiltmaking patterns and fabrics in order to create an original with a particular mood in picture form.

Plate 75 *Australis* Fiona Gavens, Whiteman Creek, NSW
DESCRIPTION: 185 × 205 cm; mixed fabrics; machine pieced and quilted

I wanted to emphasise, through my use of colour, the enormous diversity of landscape,
vegetation and climate in this country. The blurred image, as well as abstracting the map
somewhat, conveys a movement between past, present and future. It was important to balance the need for maximum colour change against the rigours of sewing hundreds of tight
curves.

Plate 76 *The Six Faces of Australia* Berys Venn-Brown, Mooloolah, Qld
DESCRIPTION: 240 × 150 cm; cotton, wool, lace, raw silk; hand and machine pieced, hand applique

With this quilt there has been a divergence from my previous work. Until recently I have been intensely interested in the Amish quilt and its disciplined approach, but with this quilt I have expressed myself. I wanted the viewer to see Australia; it has a grandeur and a wholeness that we can sometimes forget.

Plate 77 *The Australian Wild Flower Quilt* Elsie Morrison, Sydney, NSW
DESCRIPTION: 238 × 244 cm; chintz, cotton, polycotton, silk; 'stained glass window' technique, hand stitched, embroidered

This quilt was made as a memorial to my grandmother, my mother and aunts who grew up in the bush in the last century. They all had a great love of flowers as well as a strong practical and creative sense. I was most interested in getting the right colours, hence a variety of fabrics were used; each state and territory is represented in the choice of flowers.

Plate 78 *Spring Bouquets* Wendy Smith, Sydney, NSW
DESCRIPTION: 225 × 183 cm; cotton; applique using cardboard templates

I have a great love of applique and this is a continuation of past work. It started with the smaller blocks built around the fabric in the sashings which is a favourite shade of dusty pink. Owing to a particular love of medallion quilts, the centre panel was developed from a series of inspirational ideas.

Plate 79 *Unchanging Hues* Dianne Johnston, Kingaroy, Qld
DESCRIPTION: 285 × 285 cm; cotton, polycotton; machine pieced, hand applique and quilted

The flowers in the mixed sprays are all the Australian state wild flower emblems, plus the
Australian Capital Territory bluebell and the Australian wattle. I have also included a small
border of wattle and eucalypts, because they are so much a part of our heritage. Colour was
all important. Many of the flowers have been padded to add another level to the quilt, and
I have added 'floating' petals and leaves to break the usual flat look of applique.

Plate 80 *Starry Eyes* Margot Child, Sydney, NSW
DESCRIPTION: 220 × 195 cm; cotton; hand pieced and quilted

I like the evocative nature of fabrics and the peaceful nature of the stitching, which I mostly
do by hand. Time is not important to me. The decorative aspect is all important. My work
is in the folk art tradition — meant for beds.

101

Plate 81 *Delicate Balance* Christa Roksandic, Canberra, ACT
DESCRIPTION: 300 × 300 cm; cotton, cotton blends, polyester, taffeta, silk; machine pieced, hand quilted

I deliberately include very large pieces of fabric with the intention of doing involved surface quilting later on. This can add movement, depth and extensions to the design. I outline all my piecing and then use surface quilting to achieve a special effect — like the water moving in and out of the bay, or the cliffs disappearing in the distance.

Plate 82 *Sydney Harbour on a Sunday Afternoon* Trudy Billingsley, Sydney, NSW
DESCRIPTION: 200 × 220 cm; silk, satin, lurex, organza, cotton; applique, beaded, quilted

Quiltmaking is a means of recording and remembering special events in my life. One Sunday afternoon we had a wonderful walk in the Botanical Gardens where I made some sketches. It is the colours which give the time and setting to my work. This quilt was designed to be a warm, dry day with wind, and bright light to show off the flowers and harbour at its best.

Plate 83 *Journey To* Hilda Farquhar-Smith, Sydney, NSW
DESCRIPTION: 181 × 152 cm; cotton, polycotton; machine pieced, hand quilted

I set out to create the feeling of moving through life with its highs and lows, light and dark periods. The quilting, an important integral part of the whole, reinforces the feeling of movement.

New Year's Day

Australia Day

Show Day

Labour Day

Anzac Day

Easter

Melbourne Cup Day

Queen's Birthday

Christmas

Boxing Day

Plate 84 *Australia — Land of the Long Weekend* Jane Lambert, Linda McGuire, Joan Morton, Beverley McDonald, Janelle Brown, Brisbane, Qld
DESCRIPTION: 10 panels, each 75 × 60 cm; cotton, synthetic, lurex, felt, leather; machine pieced, hand and machine applique, embroidered and quilted

There are ten public holidays celebrated nationally within Australia each year. The historical aspect, shown for each particular holiday, and the activities and pastimes we all enjoy are an expression of our way of life, and how we spend a great deal of our leisure time.

105

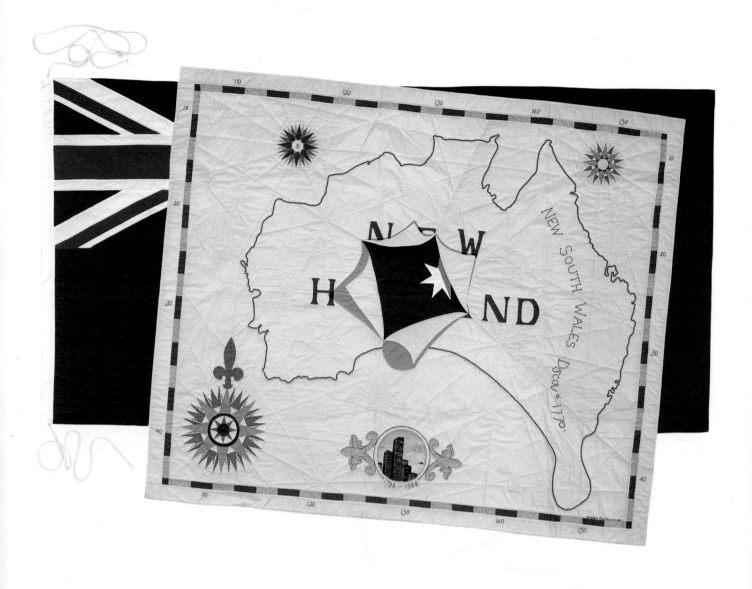

Plate 85 *Past, Present and Future* Waverley Patchworkers, Melbourne, Vic
DESCRIPTION: 163 × 234 cm; cotton; hand and machine pieced, applique, hand quilted

The fabric was tea-dyed to show an old sea chart, and an authentic map of 1790 was our
inspiration. Mariners' compasses were pieced and quilting lines were planned to criss-cross
the chart. Quilted figures were added: Captain Cook, Governor Phillip, an Aborigine and our
wildlife — kangaroos, emu, a kookaburra, a lizard, a koala and a platypus.

Plate 86 *Two Hundred Years of Australian History* Jane Wilson, Brisbane, Qld
DESCRIPTION: 250 × 250 cm; cotton, polycotton; machine pieced and embroidered, hand applique and quilted

This quilt is much more ambitious than previous work. Instead of following only one idea it developed seven aspects of the one idea. It is a breakthrough too in the scale of the project and the complexity of the colour.

Plate 87 *Spirit of Australia* Helen Zoch, Sydney, NSW
DESCRIPTION: 180 × 154 cm; cotton, polycotton, wool, silk; hand pieced, applique, quilted

This is my first finished quilt. I could not envisage a quilt about Australia without the sun.
The colours I used extended themselves to the Aboriginal inspired designs around the quilt.
The rays of the sun radiate over the whole quilt.

Plate 88 *Breaking of the Drought* Kathy O'Neill, Penrith, NSW
DESCRIPTION: 147 × 154 cm; lawn, poplin, nylon blends and other fabrics; strip pieced, applique

Drought can cause havoc both on the land and with people's emotions. The images in this quilt are of extreme heat; the yellows, reds, oranges like a heat haze. The blues, greys, and blacks are storm clouds, heavy with rain that will bring new life to the earth.

Plate 89 *Bicentennial Banner* Helen Macartney, Sydney, NSW
DESCRIPTION: 180 × 250 cm; cotton, linen, acetate flats; machine pieced, applique, hand quilted
Photography by Karl Schwerdtfeger

Working intuitively with fabric is when I'm happiest. I think it provides a kind of freedom, and definitely keeps me sane.

110

P O S T S C R I P T :

T H E   F I R E

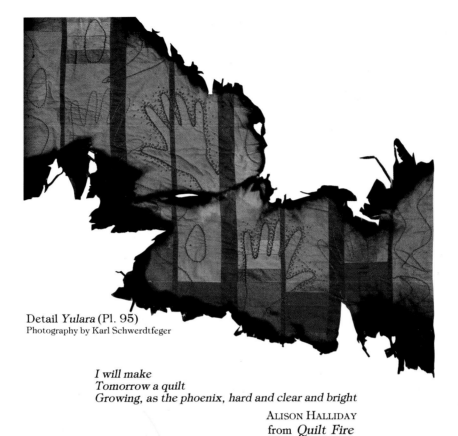

Detail *Yulara* (Pl. 95)
Photography by Karl Schwerdtfeger

I will make
Tomorrow a quilt
Growing, as the phoenix, hard and clear and bright

ALISON HALLIDAY
from *Quilt Fire*

In November 1987, a group of the exhibition quilts were gathered from around Australia to be photographed for *Quilt Australia*. Tragically, there was a fire at the photographer's studio and seventeen of the quilts which had yet to be photographed, were burnt.

As news of the disaster spread condolences came in from all over Australia. Other quiltmakers spontaneously offered fabrics as an incentive for those affected to start again. From my experience, the fabrics that I was given have suggested several new directions to explore. So although my original quilt cannot be reproduced the ideas that were important to it can be extended.

The recurring reaction of those whose quilts had been burnt was an incredulous 'but my life was in that quilt'. Cherished fabrics and associations, as well as the huge effort, some-times hundreds of hours, had gone into the quilts. Although most of the damaged quilts have not been photographed professionally, they are reproduced here as faithfully as possible, using amateur photographs.

Some quiltmakers have been able to substitute another of their quilts in the main body of the book. For others, it will take many months to make a replacement for the exhibition, so these do not appear in the book. Everyone shares in the loss.

DIANNE FINNEGAN

Plate 90 *Mottlecah* Elsie Morrison, Sydney, NSW
DESCRIPTION: 250 × 228 cm; cotton, polycotton; hand pieced and applique

The Mottlecah, or *Eucalyptus macrocarpa* is an endangered species of mallee gum found only in two restricted habitats of Western Australia — a narrow zone north of Geraldton, and into the wheat belt. It has the largest flowers and the broadest fruit of the eucalypts. Owners of private land where the tree grows have been asked to aid in its preservation and conservation.

Plate 91 *Dreamtime — Land and Sea* Holly Pittman, Brisbane, Qld
DESCRIPTION: 220 × 200 cm; mixed fabrics; pieced, applique, reverse applique, quilted

Inspired by Aboriginal bark paintings, I developed my concept by means of sketches on paper which included layouts, colours and finely quilted designs. The quilt is, in many respects, a scrap quilt with over 144 different fabrics used.

112

Plate 92 *Dubbo Bicentennial Quilt* Dubbo Patchwork and Quilters Group, Dubbo, NSW
DESCRIPTION: 313 × 238 cm; cotton, linen, silk, furnishing fabric, velvet, knits; machine and hand pieced, hand applique, embroidered, hand quilted   Photography by Karl Schwerdtfeger

Although Dubbo is a city of some 33,000 people, known as the 'hub of the West' and situated on the banks of the Macquarie River, the quilt depicts the surrounding isolation of larger rural properties from which some of our membership is drawn, uniting city and country people in a common bond. Dubbo is well known for its historic buildings and the Western Plains Zoo.

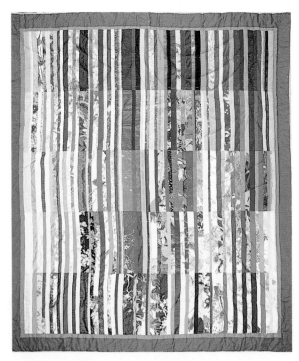

Plate 93 *Rosefield* Sally Evers, Hobart, Tas
DESCRIPTION: 222 × 196 cm; cotton, polycotton, silk; machine pieced, hand quilted

If, by choosing a certain style to illustrate a theme (sunlight filtering through the tangle of trees, shrubs and flowers in my garden), I can create a bit of mystery and magic that touches the viewer's imagination, then that is a wonderful bonus.

Plate 94 *Warrumbungle Dream Time* D. Anne Neal, Corindi Beach, NSW
DESCRIPTION: 250 × 197 cm; cotton, polycotton, fabric paint; machine and hand pieced, applique, embroidered, quilted

I paint, but usually find the medium of paint lacking in texture and depth, so increasingly my paintings are being interpreted in thread and fabric.

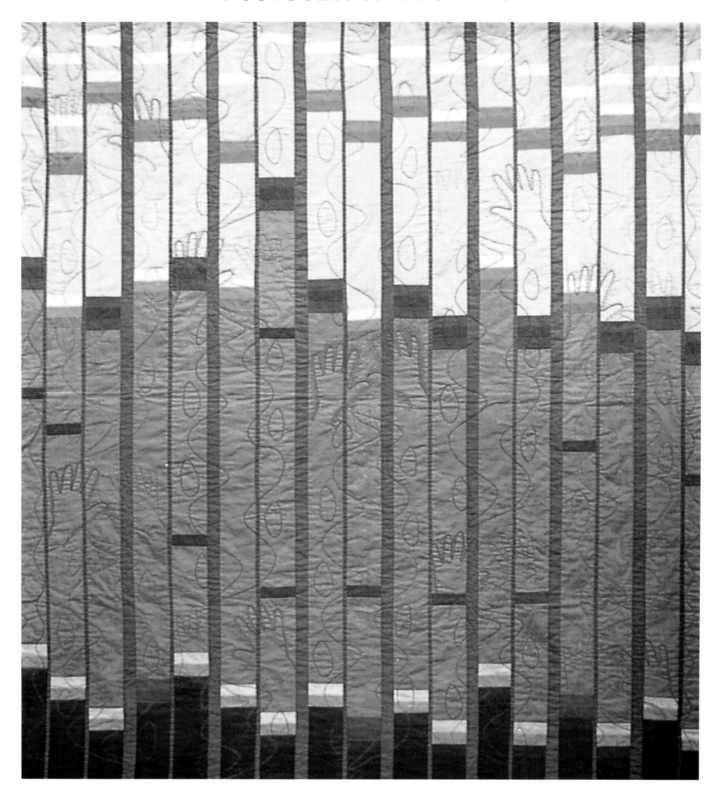

Plate 95 *Yulara* Prue Socha, Sydney, NSW
DESCRIPTION: 212 × 198 cm; cotton; machine pieced, hand embroidered, quilted   Photography by Sylvie Picot

A couple of years ago I made an exciting visit to central Australia. I have tried to capture the space, colour and light of that area in this quilt.

115

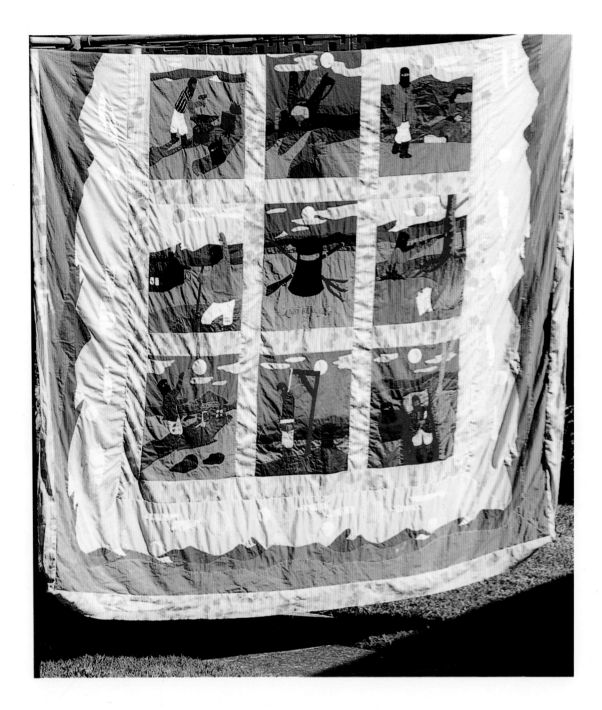

Plate 96 *My Life and Hard Times by Ned Kelly* Judith Fluke and Roy Fluke, Sydney, NSW
DESCRIPTION: 240 × 200 cm; cotton homespun; applique, quilted

We have combined our talents as artist and quiltmaker to conceive a work that has perspective and colour and tells a story. My father-in-law, Roy, who is foremost a painter, has always been interested in pure design and found that he could apply these principles to creating a quilt.

Plate 97 *Postscript to the Dreaming* Crazy Cooperative, Melbourne, Vic
DESCRIPTION: 270 × 190 cm; cotton; machine and hand pieced, hand dyed, painted, embroidered, hand quilted

In this quilt we have represented Australia before European settlement in a quilted background of flora and fauna, and then overlaid picture blocks of images associated with the history of Australia since 1788.

Plate 98 *Wild Flowers of Australia* Marie Parnell, Sydney, NSW
DESCRIPTION: 265 × 265 cm; cotton, silk, organza; shadow applique, quilted

As I am unskilled in sewing, each completed piece of work gives me a wonderful sense of satisfaction. I also enjoy flower arranging — maybe that is why I love to quilt floral designs.

Plate 99 *Birthday Garland* Wendy Saclier and Vivienne Mildren, Canberra, ACT
DESCRIPTION: 250 × 220 cm; cotton, polycotton; hand applique, embroidered, quilted

This is the fifth quilt Vivienne and I have made together and it is the culmination of our exploration of representational technique. As Vivienne lives in Ulladulla and I live in Canberra quilt bits are transported to and fro during the making process. We both delight in the beauty of Australian flowers.

Plate 100 *The Barrier Reef Quilt* Cynthia Morgan, Caloundra, Qld
DESCRIPTION: 255 × 205 cm; cotton, silk, polyester; hand dyed, painted, machine embroidered, quilted

When snorkelling on Heron Island, the sight of the myriads of colourful fish darting in and out of the coral entranced me. I wanted to capture this movement against the background of coral and the blue of the sea. We have to learn to live with our natural heritage and take care to preserve and protect it.

Plate 101 *Woman's Mirror* Lois Densham, Melbourne, Vic
DESCRIPTION: 220 × 180 cm; recycled linen, personal objects; tacking, machine pieced, hand quilted

This quilt is one of a pair — the companion to the man's quilt which showed him surrounded by people. The *Woman's Mirror* shows the woman at the centre. She has to be self-sufficient in giving support to those around her. It is made up of the clothing of the '50s and represents my generation, family life and love.

Plate 102 *Opals* Barbara Macey, Melbourne, Vic
DESCRIPTION: 165 × 155 cm; cotton, satin, taffeta, organza; machine pieced

I have been exploring the log cabin mode since 1972. This quilt follows from two previous crazy patchwork quilts made in 1985. The construction methods are closely related but the less formal, crazy style allows greater freedom of form and colour.

Plate 103 *Whispering Waters* Phyllis Sullivan, Blackmans Bay, Tas
DESCRIPTION: 221 × 197 cm; cotton, cotton blends; machine pieced, hand quilted

This quilt is a continuation of a previous work using the negative of curved two patch. Playing with stripped piecing on curved seams taught me some interesting things.

Plate 104 *Nandalie* Phyllis Sullivan, Blackmans Bay, Tas
DESCRIPTION: 258 × 258 cm; cotton, cotton blends; machine pieced, hand quilted

This quilt is a remembrance of our devastating bush fires. The fire, shown by the curved two patched system, was the inspiration — the rest grew from there.

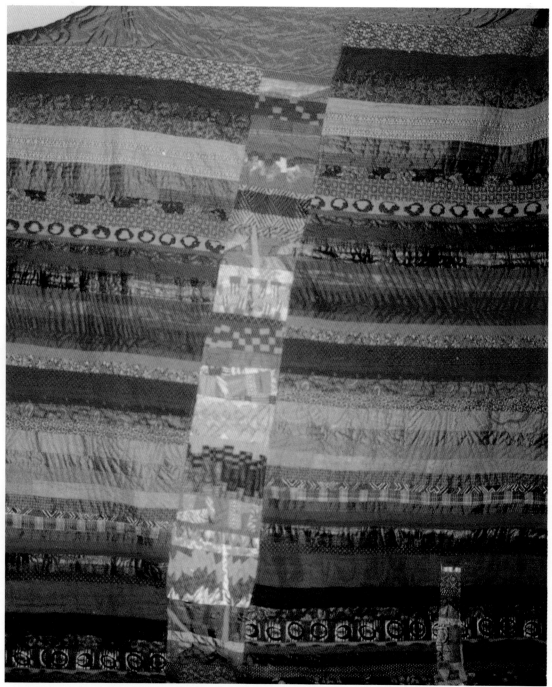

Plate 105 *Dislocation* Dianne Finnegan, Sydney, NSW
DESCRIPTION: 262 × 210 cm; cotton, silk, linen and blends; machine pieced and quilted, hand applique
(Photograph of work in progress)

Quiltmaking has alerted me to the fact that many decisions in life can be solved creatively, and with some thought to good design. My background is in geomorphology, which, like quiltmaking, explores the interrelationships of shapes.

LIST OF PLATES

LIST OF QUILTMAKERS

In order of appearance:

ELIZABETH MACARTHUR (attrib.),
  Parramatta, NSW
MRS BROWN, Bowning, NSW
MARY HINDE, Sydney, NSW
VAL NADIN, Sydney, NSW
PAMELA TIMMINS, Sydney, NSW
JENNIFER LEWIS, Melbourne, Vic
NARELLE GRIEVE, Sydney, NSW
WENDY WYCHERLEY, Perth, WA
HELEN MACARTNEY, Sydney, NSW
CAROL IRELAND, New Town, Tas
GEORGINA CHILD, Colorado, USA
DIANA GOULSTON ROBINSON, New York,
  USA
JUDY HOOWORTH, Sydney, NSW
SUE ROWLEY, Wollongong, NSW
JANE MITCHELL, Fremantle, WA
WENDY HOLLAND, Sydney, NSW
SANDY WARD, Melbourne, Vic
TRUDY BILLINGSLEY, Sydney, NSW
THE QUILTERS' GUILD OF SOUTH
  AUSTRALIA, Adelaide, SA
BARBARA RADZEVICIUS, Sydney, NSW
CANBERRA BLUEBELL QUILTERS, Canberra,
  ACT
STAR OF THE SEA COLLEGE, Melbourne, Vic
JAN FRAZER, Melbourne, Vic
MARGARET MACCIONI, Sydney, NSW
LINDA STERN, Melbourne, Vic
MARJORIE COLEMAN, Perth, WA
WAGGA WAGGA QUILTERS GROUP, Wagga
  Wagga, NSW
EDITH HIGGINS, Bullaburra, NSW
LUCY HILL, Caloundra, Qld
JENNIE STEVENS, Canberra, ACT
JAN IRVINE, Sydney, NSW
HELEN SLOCOMBE, Sydney, NSW
LOIS DENSHAM, Melbourne, Vic
YVONNE CHAPMAN, Valley Heights, NSW
IRMA CHELSWORTH, The Channon via
  Lismore, NSW
JUDY TURNER, Canberra, ACT
PEEL COTTAGE QUILTERS, Tamworth,
  NSW

ALISON MUIR, Sydney, NSW
WENDY LUGG, Perth, WA
BEVERLEY SACH, Canberra, ACT
JILL VANDERKOOI, Blaxland, NSW
BATIK ASSOCIATION OF ACT, Canberra,
  ACT
CYNTHIA MORGAN, Brisbane, Qld
SALLY EVERS, Hobart, Tas
BETTY BROWN, Kettering, Tas
JOY WOODGATE, Sydney, NSW
DIANA THOMAS, Sydney, NSW
KAREN FAIL, Sydney, NSW
FELICITY NAESS, Hazelbrook, NSW
JENNY MARTYN, Melbourne, Vic
SUSAN BLANCHFIELD, Jamberoo, NSW
GREG SOMERVILLE, Lawson, NSW
KAREN ALLISON, Devonport, Tas
PAMELA TAWTON, Canberra, ACT
SUSAN DENTON, Melbourne, Vic
FIBRE FIVE, Canberra, ACT
PERRY MCINTYRE, Sydney, NSW
LORRAINE HEPBURN, Sydney, NSW
YOLANDA GIFFORD, Sydney, NSW
PIMPAMA PATCHWORKERS, Pimpama, Qld
SALLY ASTRIDGE, Sydney, NSW
LAURELL BROWN, Launceston, Tas
BARBARA MACEY, Melbourne, Vic
NANCY TINGEY, Canberra, ACT
STUDENTS OF YEAR 7, 1987, Caroline
  Chisholm High School, Canberra, ACT
ANN HADDAD, Canberra, ACT
AMERICAN WOMEN OF SYDNEY, Sydney,
  NSW
CHRISTINE LING, Blackwater, Qld
THE YANKALILLA QUILTING COMMUNITY,
  SA
INDOOROOPILLY QUILTERS, Brisbane, Qld
YVONNE LINE, Sydney, NSW
KERRY BEAUMONT, Hazelbrook, NSW
FIONA GAVENS, Whiteman Creek, NSW
BERYS VENN-BROWN, Mooloolah, Qld
ELSIE MORRISON, Sydney, NSW
WENDY SMITH, Sydney, NSW
DIANNE JOHNSTON, Kingaroy, Qld
MARGOT CHILD, Sydney, NSW

CHRISTA ROKSANDIC, Canberra, ACT
HILDA FARQUHAR-SMITH, Sydney, NSW
JANE LAMBERT, Brisbane, Qld
LINDA MCGUIRE, Brisbane, Qld
JOAN MORTON, Brisbane, Qld
BEVERLEY MCDONALD, Brisbane, Qld
JANELLE BROWN, Brisbane, Qld
WAVERLEY PATCHWORKERS, Melbourne,
  Vic
JANE WILSON, Brisbane, Qld
HELEN ZOCH, Sydney, NSW
KATHY O'NEILL, Penrith, NSW
HOLLY PITTMAN, Brisbane, Qld
DUBBO PATCHWORK AND QUILTERS GROUP,
  Dubbo, NSW:
    FAY BIFHOFF
    CHARLENE BOWER
    ELIZABETH CHARLSTON
    MEG CORISH
    JANICE GARTH
    CIS HONNER
    SUZANNE LAIRD
    LOUISE MARTEL
    CHERYL PRATTER
    NAOMI RAISON
    ALICIA RAWSON
    SUSAN TOOTH
    JULIE VAUGHN
    JOANNE WEBB
D. ANNE NEAL, Corindi Beach, NSW
PRUE SOCHA, Sydney, NSW
JUDITH FLUKE, Sydney, NSW
ROY FLUKE, Sydney, NSW
CRAZY COOPERATIVE, Melbourne, Vic:
    SUE BACH
    RUTH CAPLE
    CHRISTINE CEMM
    DOROTHY DE NYS
    MARLE POPPLE
    JOS TOLSON
MARIE PARNELL, Sydney, NSW
WENDY SACLIER, Canberra, ACT
VIVIENNE MILDREN, Ulladulla, NSW
PHYLLIS SULLIVAN, Blackmans Bay, Tas
DIANNE FINNEGAN, Sydney, NSW

BIBLIOGRAPHY

ANTMANN, GISELLE 'Signs; Janice Irvine's Quilts' *Craft Australia*, 1985, 4

BREARLEY, DEBORAH *Patches of Australia: A Selection of Patchwork, Applique and Quilting Patterns*, Edward Arnold, Victoria, 1985

COOPER, ROBYN & OUTTERIDGE, ADELE 'Precious Little Scraps' *Craft Australia Winter Supplement*, 1984, 2

'Geometric Tableaux' *Craft Arts*, 1985, 2

DENTON, SUSAN & MACEY, BARBARA *Quiltmaking*, Thomas Nelson Australia, Melbourne, 1987

GERO, ANNETTE 'Quilts and Their Makers in Nineteenth-Century Australia' *The Quilt Digest*, 5, ed. M. M. Kile, The Quilt Digest Press, San Francisco, 1987

GERO, ANNETTE & HOLLAND, WENDY 'The Quiltmakers' Art' *Craft Arts*, 1986, 6

HERSEY, APRIL 'Design Section: Quilts Elizabeth (*sic*) Kruger' *Craft Australia*, 1979, 3

IRVINE, JANICE 'Interpreting an Old Craft' *Craft in Australia* ed. A. Moult, Reed Books, Frenchs Forest, NSW, 1984

MARSH, GLENNDA 'Quilts in Women's Lives — The Australian Post-War Revival'. A paper delivered at the Australian National University, 18 August, 1987

ROLFE, MARGARET *Australian Patchwork: A Step-by-Step Guide to Piecing, Quilting & Applique* Currey O'Neil, Victoria, 1985

Quilt a Koala: Australian animals and birds in patchwork Wattle Books, Melbourne, 1986

Patchwork Quilts in Australia Greenhouse Publications, Victoria, 1987

'Her own precise way; Barbara Macey' *Craft Australia* 1987, 1